Facts About the Reindeer

By Lisa Strattin

© 2019 Lisa Strattin

FREE BOOK

FREE FOR ALL SUBSCRIBERS

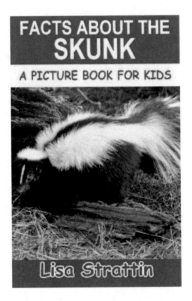

LisaStrattin.com/Subscribe-Here

BOX SET

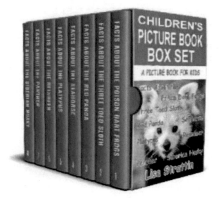

- **FACTS ABOUT THE POISON DART FROGS**
- **FACTS ABOUT THE THREE TOED SLOTH**
- **FACTS ABOUT THE RED PANDA**
- **FACTS ABOUT THE SEAHORSE**
- **FACTS ABOUT THE PLATYPUS**
- **FACTS ABOUT THE REINDEER**
- **FACTS ABOUT THE PANTHER**
- **FACTS ABOUT THE SIBERIAN HUSKY**

LisaStrattin.com/BookBundle

Facts for Kids Picture Books by Lisa Strattin

Sign Up for New Release Emails Here

LisaStrattin.com/subscribe-here

COVER IMAGE

https://flickr.com/photos/timo_w2s/6014343165/

ADDITIONAL IMAGES

https://flickr.com/photos/mrfraley/5337570375/

https://flickr.com/photos/timo_w2s/3942143718/

https://flickr.com/photos/timo_w2s/3942150036/

https://flickr.com/photos/timo_w2s/2484479448/

https://flickr.com/photos/timo_w2s/28645886946/

https://flickr.com/photos/oddwick/3581966839/

https://flickr.com/photos/lalouque/3881523236/

https://flickr.com/photos/133552319@N08/18131266352/

https://flickr.com/photos/alban-py/48367701516/

https://flickr.com/photos/mrfraley/44687487630/

Contents

INTRODUCTION

The reindeer, also known as the caribou, is found in large herds in the very north part of the world. Reindeer live in the Arctic Tundra and the North Pole regions which include parts of North America, Europe and Asia.

The reindeer's hooves adjust to the season, so in the summer when the tundra is soft and wet, the reindeer's footpads become soft and sponge-like in order to get a bigger footprint on the damp ground. In the winter, the reindeer's footpads shrink and tighten, allowing the rim of the hoof to cut into the ice and crusted snow in order to keep the reindeer from slipping.

CHARACTERISTICS

Male reindeer lose their antlers in November, but females keep theirs much longer. (This means that Santa Claus' reindeer must have all been female, since they are always shown having horns on December 24.)

They are built for the cold. Their noses warm up the air before it gets to their lungs and their entire bodies, including their hooves, are covered with fur.

They are very social creatures. They feed, travel and rest in groups called herds. These herds can be from 10 animals to a few hundred in a herd. In the spring, herds get even bigger, growing to be as many as 50,000 to 500,000 members!

The herds often travel south as much as 1,000 miles to 3,000 miles to find food in the winter.

APPEARANCE

Reindeer don't fly, but they do sometimes have red noses. Reindeer have 25 percent more capillaries (blood vessels) carrying red, oxygen-rich blood in their nasal architecture than humans, so when it gets cold, their noses get red!

Like others in the deer family, reindeers have long legs, hooves and antlers.

LIFE STAGES

Females have a gestation period of about 7.5 months and typically give birth to only one baby at a time, though there have been records of up to four young at a time. A baby reindeer is called a calf.

Calves are able to stand about an hour after they are born, and within a week they start eating grasses and other vegetation in addition to their mother's milk. They are weaned when they are six months old and start growing their first set of antlers around their second birthday. Reindeers are considered to be adults at 4 to 6 years old.

LIFE SPAN

Reindeer live, on average, 12-15 years.

SIZE

Adult reindeer grow to be 5 to 6 feet tall and weigh 130 to 700 pounds.

HABITAT

Reindeer are found in Alaska, Canada, Greenland, northern Europe and northern Asia in tundra, mountains and woodland habitats. Their home ranges tend be as big as 190 square miles, although when searching for food in winter they may travel very far from their home range.

DIET

Reindeer are herbivores, which means they only eat plants. Their diet can include herbs, ferns, mosses, grasses, shoots, fungi, berries and leaves. On average, an adult reindeer eats around 9 to 18 pounds of vegetation a day.

In the winter, reindeer must dig deep into the snow to find food. They use their antlers to do this and also munch on energy-packed lichens called reindeer moss.

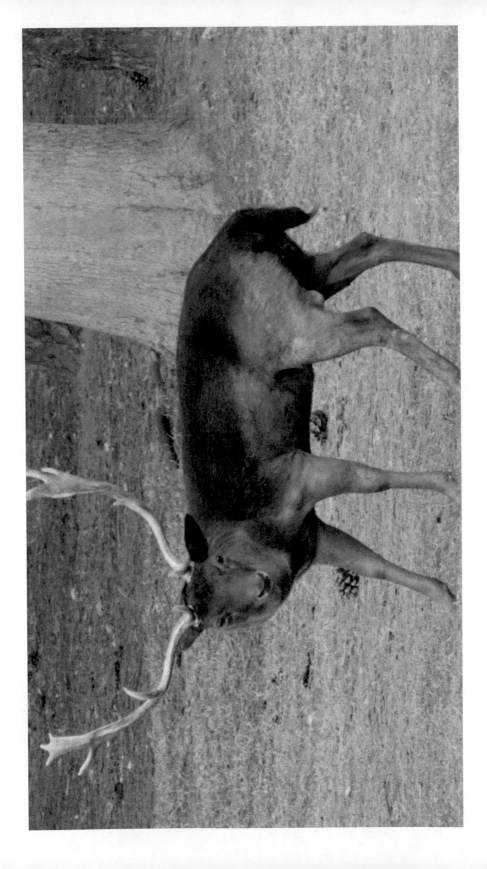

ENEMIES

The reindeer is often a target for the large predators that exist in the Arctic Circle, however the reindeer is a very fast runner and moves in large herds so it is not easy to catch.

Arctic wolves, polar bears, brown bears and humans are predators that hunt the reindeer.

SUITABILITY AS PETS

Of course, the reindeer is not a suitable pet. They are very large and need to be able to roam around and run free. You can visit reindeer at many zoos, so if you want to see them, this is a good choice for you.

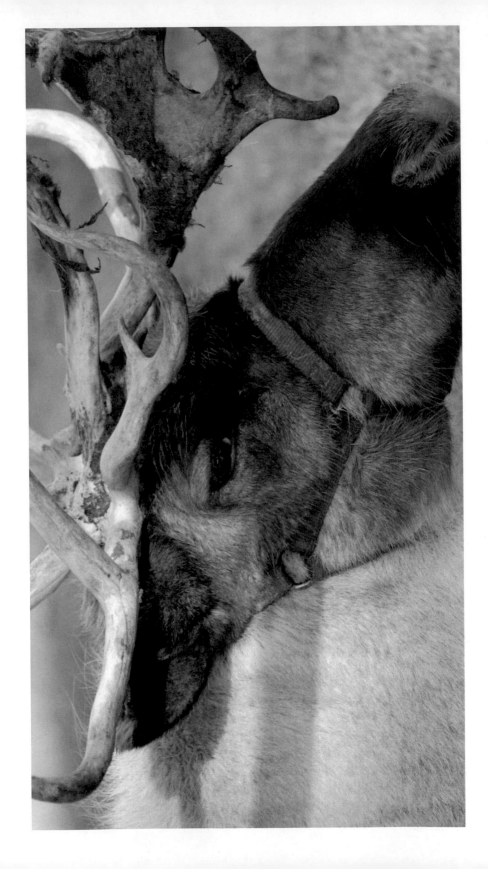

COLOR ME

COLOR ME

COLOR ME

COLOR ME

COLOR ME

COLOR ME

COLOR ME

Please leave me a review here:

LisaStrattin.com/Review-Vol-211

For more Kindle Downloads Visit Lisa Strattin Author Page on Amazon Author Central

amazon.com/author/lisastrattin

To see upcoming titles, visit my website at LisaStrattin.com– most books available on Kindle!

LisaStrattin.com

FREE BOOK

FOR ALL SUBSCRIBERS – SIGN UP NOW

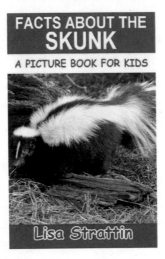

LisaStrattin.com/Subscribe-Here

LisaStrattin.com/Facebook

LisaStrattin.com/Youtube